Marie Galante Island Travel and Tourism

Vacation, Holiday, Honeymoon

Author
Gabriel Cole

Copyright Notice

Copyright © 2017 Global Print Digital
All Rights Reserved

Digital Management Copyright Notice. This Title is not in public domain, it is copyrighted to the original author, and being published by **Global Print Digital**. No other means of reproducing this title is accepted, and none of its content is editable, neither right to commercialize it is accepted, except with the consent of the author or authorized distributor. You must purchase this Title from a vendor who's right is given to sell it, other sources of purchase are not accepted, and accountable for an action against. We are happy that you understood, and being guided by these terms as you proceed. Thank you

First Printing: 2017.

ISBN: 978-1-912483-07-5

Publisher: Global Print Digital.
Arlington Row, Bibury, Cirencester GL7 5ND
Gloucester
United Kingdom.
Website: www.homeworkoffer.com

Table of Content

Touristic Introduction 1
History 3
Travel and Tourism 9
   Accommodations.. 12
      Marie Galante Hotels 14
   Transportation 39
      Air Travel 43
      Rental Cars 47
      Sailing & Boating 49
      Taxis 52
   Guide to Marie Galante.. 55
      How to Get There.. 55
      Where to stay.. 56
      When to Go 58
      Tourist Info 58
      Travel Information 59
   Sightseeing and things to do 61
      Shopping 67
   Restaurant... 68
      Le Touloulou 72
      Manman'dlo La Sirene 74
      Le Maria-Galanda 76
   Activities 80
      Diving 82
         Ti'bulles Dive Center 84
         Man'balaou Club de Plongee 85
      Snorkeling 87
   Attractions... 89
      Museum 94
      Beaches 95
         Plage de Folle Anse 98
         Petite-Anse 104
         Anse Feuillard 111
         Anse de l'Eglise 118
         Anse Canot.. 125

Touristic Introduction

Welcome to Marie-Galante

This enchanting island still remains one of the best-kept secrets in the Caribbean. Fortunate visitors to Marie-Galante will discover rolling green hills, turquoise lagoons, picturesque villages and spectacular beaches.

Visitors will feel they have moved back in time to an era of charming architecture, nineteenth century windmills and colorful markets. Traditional oxcarts can be seen bringing in crops from the cane fields. This is a place of mystical beauty with lush greenery and fascinating historical sites such as the 18th century Château Murat.

Marie-Galante is a perfect island to explore by car, scooter, mountain-bike or hiking. Located about 30 km (18 miles) south of Guadeloupe, the magic of the true Caribbean and its rural traditions await within its circular coastline.

Please use the drop-down MARIE-GALANTE menu above or the links below to find out more. We're looking forward to sharing this sensational destination with you

History

The origins of Marie Galante.

The oldest known civilization that occupied the territory of Marie Galante was the Huécoïdes. They were followed by the Arawaks and around the year 850 by the Caribbean.

The arrival of Christophe Colomb

Marie-Galante is the first island of the Guadeloupean archipelago that Christophe COLOMB reached on his second trip. The explorer landed at a place called "Anse Ballet" in Grand-Bourg 3 November 1493. He gave the island, which was called by the Caribbean and Aichi

Touloukaéra by the Arawaks, the name of its flagship "Maria-Galanda ".

The first French settlers

The Governor HOUEL, organized November 8, 1648 the establishment of the first French settlers, fifty men, near the place called Old Fort in St. Louis. On 4 September 1649, Jacques de BOISSERET bought the island to the American Islands Company. In 1653, the few settlers who had not yielded to discouragement to the harsh living conditions were massacred by the Caribbean rapes retaliation in Dominica by marine barge came from Martinique.

Implantation of sugarcane

Sugar cane, probably originated in India and imported by Christophe COLOMB in the West Indies, was cultivated in Guadeloupe for its industrialization from 1654 through settlers expelled from Brazil that generate the creation of the first sweets dwellings equipped a small mill animals (carousel) for crushing the cane. 1660 saw the signing, on Castle Basse-Terre, the peace treaty with the Caribbean than the French and English allow to settle on Dominica and St. Vincent. The island being "pacified", technological and human conditions are ripe for the development of the market economy based on the home as a production unit and the labor of black slaves imported from Africa.

In 1664, Madame de BOISSERET assigned its rights to the West India Company. Island then had its first 4 mills (mills beasts). In 1665, his son Monsieur BOISSERET of Téméricourt became governor. The map of the island it establishes bears his coat of arms.

The island was sacked by the Dutch in June 1676, followed by the English in 1690 and 1691. Following these looting that led to the destruction of the mills, sweets and from the population, the repopulation of the island was banned by the Governor of Martinique until 1696. the British occupied the island again from 1759 to 1763. old candy Murat.

Windmills appeared in 1780. In 1830 there were up to 105 mills which more than half were still operated by oxen.

Aujourd'hui 72 tours de moulins sont encore visibles.

Abolition de l'esclavage

De novembre 1792 jusqu'en 1794, Marie-Galante devient indépendante pour s'affranchir d'une Guadeloupe royaliste.

L'esclavage, qui fut une première fois aboli en 1794 et rétabli en 1802, fut définitivement aboli en 1848 grâce à l'action conjuguée des abolitionnistes, tel que Victor SCHOELCHER, et des révoltes incessantes des nègres esclaves. La première participation des nouveaux affranchis aux élections législatives les 24 et 25 juin

1849 fut marquée par la répression sanglante des mouvements de protestation de la majorité de la population contre les tentatives de fraudes électorales orchestrées par les grands planteurs blancs. Des dizaines de nègres furent tués pendant ces événements qui conduisirent au déversement du rhum et du sucre de l'habitation Pirogue dans la mare à proximité, aujourd'hui appelée " la mare au punch " en mémoire de ces évènements tragiques.

Département français

L'archipel Guadeloupéen constitué principalement des îles Grande-Terre, Basse-Terre, Marie-Galante, Saint-Martin, Saint-Barthélemy, Terre de Haut, Terre de Bas et la Désirade est un Département français depuis 1946 et une Région monodépartementale depuis 1982.

Les trois Communes que compte Marie-Galante - Capesterre, Grand-Bourg et Saint-Louis - sont constituées en Communauté de Communes depuis le 08 janvier 1994, c'est la première des DOM.

Travel and Tourism

Ever since Christopher Columbus caught sight of Marie-Galante and named the island after his ship, the *Maria Galanda*, visitors have been captivated by this enchanting isle. Today, Marie-Galante's unspoiled scenery can be found everywhere, from its quaint chateaus to its isolated sands. And its rolling hills frosted with powdery sands, sugar plantations, and 19th-century windmills add to its rustic ambiance.

Your first stop should be Grand-Bourg, the island's main settlement (located at the southwestern tip of the island) where you'll find a helpful visitor center. From there, head south to tour the Château Murat, a famed 18th-century plantation that features an exhibit detailing the island's history of sugar cane cultivation and rum-making. The chateau welcomes visitors from around 9:15 a.m. to 5 p.m. daily, and admission is free. From here, continue south to Petite-Anse, a golden beach sheltered by sea-grape trees and Le Touloulou, a favored Creole restaurant.

Some visitors suggest carving out a day or two (at least) to explore Marie-Galante. "A half-day (8:00 am to 4:00 pm on the island) is doable to see the main highlights but an overnight stay is recommended Life is slower and quieter on this island!"

Land rural traditions.

Marie-Galante, land rural traditions, which cultivates a peaceful lifestyle, maliciously abusing more than one observer and his heart beats are activated in a flash to the rhythm of the party and his family complicity. Marie-Galante today proves to be the new destination of the French Antilles. Covering an area of 158 square kilometers, the island, which is more commonly called the "big cake" in relation to its circular shape and its low relief (the highest peak, the constant dull, rises to 204m), account three municipalities and 12 410 inhabitants. Marie Galante which counted up to 106 mills is also called "the island of a hundred mills" or "Greater dependence."

The authenticity of the life of the West Indies
In addition to all the sanitary amenities one would expect from a French Department (hospitals, doctors, pharmacies, etc ..), Marie-Galante offers the authenticity of life in the Caribbean, a charm picturesque, countless white sandy beaches, lagoons fringed by coral reefs, and the serenity of living. Lin Camphorin and Trioka The island offers many accommodation possibilities homestay, villas, tourist residences, and hotels which is a 3-star.

Accommodations

Marie Galante Accommodations

Marie Galante is a beautiful, lush green island of white-sand beaches and wonderful, clear waters. It does not offer fancy hotels or lively entertainment, but there are a number of good restaurants serving creole specialities or more traditional French food. It possesses an unpretentious simplicity and a very laid-back lifestyle and is the ideal Caribbean escape for those who want to relax.

Despite its large size in area, Marie Galante keeps its tourism numbers low by advertising its status as a quiet, private getaway destination. For this reason, there is only a small number of accommodations available to guests – but not to worry. Each one is high in quality.

Hotels

There are multiple types of accommodations to pick from on the island, including a few hotels and one resort. Click on each link to read more details.

If you are organizing a sizable get-together, or are traveling with a large group, consider a group-friendly accommodation like La Rose du Brésil. The estate is dotted with bungalows where guests stay in elegance. Each is equipped to accommodate between three and five guests, but there are connecting terraces so larger parties can feel connected. The property can be found on Route du Littoral.

Coco Beach Resort is a nice property on Marie Galante. The active traveler will feel right at home at Coco Beach Resort, which has been rated a Three Star property by the official hotel authority on the island. The property is especially known for all the free activities the property encourages its guests to take advantage of. To talk to them, call (059) 097-1046.

Village de Menard is another place to consider. Located on the property of what was once an old sugar refinery, this property is at once historic and elegant, mixing both tropical and French appeal for guests who can't resist either. If you are looking to call before booking a room, do so at (059) 097-0945.

Marie Galante has many other choices too. For more details about the hotels available, read on Hotel page.

You will be able to see a full listing of accommodations for Guadeloupe Accommodation page .

From bungalows and cottages to quiet guesthouses, and even one standard hotel, the accommodation options on Marie Galante are exactly what you want when you're looking to get away.

Marie Galante Hotels

The unspoiled natural habitat of Marie Galante means that there are no towering hotels sandwiched together all over the island. What hotels do exist are generally located along the west and south coasts each with access to the beaches. They are far enough off the shore, however, that the feel that you have found your own personal island paradise is not disrupted by the comings and goings of guest after guest.

Hotels On Marie Galante

There are multiple types of hotels to choose from on the island, including at least a few hotels and one resort. Click on the link to each accommodation to read further info.

If you are planning for a special occasion, or if you're traveling as a large party, consider a group-friendly property such as La Rose du Brésil. The estate is dotted with bungalows where guests stay in elegance. Each is equipped to accommodate between three and five guests, but there are connecting terraces so larger parties can feel connected. Visitors will find them on Route du Littoral.

Coco Beach Resort is a property worth considering on Marie Galante. The apartment rooms at Coco Beach Resort are large and modern, with views of the beach. Try calling them at (059) 097-1046.

Village de Menard: Located on the property of what was once an old sugar refinery, this property is at once historic and elegant, mixing both tropical and French appeal for guests who can't resist either. If you have questions, call them at (059) 097-0945.

Additional details for the many hotel possibilities can be seen right below.

HOTELS ON MARIE GALANTE				
Name	Type	Phone Number	Star Rating	Location
Coco Beach	Resort	(059)		2.1 mi. East-Southeast of Central

Marie Galante Island Travel and Tourism

Resort		097-1046		Grand-Bourg
Hôtel La Souricière	Hotel	(059) 097-3295		3.8 mi. East of Central Grand-Bourg
Hôtel Solédad	Hotel	(059) 097-8960		Grand-Bourg, Southwestern part of Marie Galante
La Rose du Brésil	Hotel	(059) 097-4739		5.0 mi. East of Central Grand-Bourg
Le Soleil Levant	Guest house	(059) 097-3155		6.0 mi. East of Central Grand-Bourg
Résidence Cap Reva	Hotel	(059) 097-2001		6.0 mi. East of Central Grand-Bourg
Village de Menard	Cottages	(059) 097-0945		1.3 mi. North of Central Saint Louis

If you would prefer having more accommodations beyond just these, you should look at other locations. Through Guadeloupe Accommodation page in this book to find our discussion of other kinds of accommodations for Marie Galante.

Other Hotels below:

La Maison des Iles

Situated in Beauséjour in the Marie Galante Region, this detached villa features a terrace and a garden. The property is 45 km from Le Gosier and free private parking is available. Free WiFi is offered throughout the property.

The kitchen is equipped with a dishwasher and an oven, as well as a coffee machine and a kettle. A flat-screen TV is featured. Other facilities at La Maison des Iles include a year-round outdoor pool.

Sainte-Anne is 41 km from La Maison des Iles, while Saint-François is 40 km away. The nearest airport is Guadeloupe - Pôle Caraïbes Airport, 53 km from the property.

Marie Galante Island Travel and Tourism

We speak your language!

Apartment Grand Case

Located in Capesterre, Apartment Grand Case is an apartment featuring a barbecue. The air-conditioned unit is 42 km from Le Gosier.

The kitchen is equipped with an oven. A TV is available. There is a private bathroom with a shower.

Sainte-Anne is 37 km from Apartment Grand Case, while Saint-François is 36 km from the property. The nearest airport is Guadeloupe - Pôle Caraïbes Airport, 50 km from the property.

We speak your language!

Your stay will include:

 Free WiFi

Apartment Grand Case has been welcoming Booking.com guests since 13 Dec 2016.

Kaz'hamac

Kaz'hamac is located 3 km from Grand-Bourg town centre and 4.5 km from Coco Beach. Free WiFi access is available in all areas.

The rooms here will provide you with a terrace. There is a full a kitchenette with a fridge and a coffee machine. Shared bathrooms also come with a shower. You can enjoy sea view and garden view from all the rooms.

At Kaz'hamac you will find a garden, a terrace and a shared kitchen. The property offers free parking and guests can find the Chez Henri Restaurant Bar.

This property is 6 km from the local airport.

This property is also rated for the best value in Grand-Bourg! Guests are getting more for their money when compared to other properties in this city.

We speak your language!

Kaz'hamac has been welcoming Booking.com guests since 9 Jun 2014

Cap Est

Cap Est offers accommodation in Capesterre, just a 5-minute walk from La Feuillère beach. Guests benefit from balcony. Free WiFi is featured throughout the property.

There is a seating area, a dining area and a kitchen equipped with an oven. A flat-screen TV is offered. There is a private bathroom with a bath.

Le Gosier is 46 km from Cap Est, while Sainte-Anne is 41 km from the property. The nearest airport is Guadeloupe - Pôle Caraïbes Airport, 53 km from the property.

You get good value for money here, according to couples who spent time at the property. They rate it 8.0.

Villa Alizea

Villa Alizea is a villa featuring a garden with a year-round outdoor pool, located in Capesterre. It provides free private parking. Free WiFi is provided throughout the property.

The unit equipped with a kitchen with a dishwasher and oven. A flat-screen TV is offered. Other facilities at Villa Alizea include a barbecue.

Le Gosier is 45 km from Villa Alizea, while Sainte-Anne is 41 km from the property. The area is popular for diving and fishing. The nearest airport is Guadeloupe - Pôle Caraïbes Airport, 53 km from the property.

La Kallina

Located on the small island of Marie Galante, La Kallina features an outdoor swimming pool and a garden. Free private parking is available and WiFi is provided at the reception desk.

La Kallina's air-conditioned studios and bungalows are self-contained and feature a closet, TV with cable channels and a private bathroom. Some of them have a private terrace and garden view.

A variety of restaurants and bars can be found within 1.5 km from the property. Activities in the vicinity of the property include hiking, surfing, kayaking and bicycling.

Capesterre is a 10 minutes' drive, while Grand Bourg can be reached within 5 minutes. Marie Galante Airport is 5 km from the property.

We speak your language!

La Kallina has been welcoming Booking.com guests since 28 Mar 2013.

Au Village de Menard

This property is 18 minutes walk from the beach. Featuring an outdoor pool and a restaurant open for dinner and for breakfast, Au Village de Menard it's located 2 km from the old fort from the beach, 5 km from Mays and 8 km from Saint Louis village. Free Wi Fi in public areas is available.

The rooms here will provide you with a TV, air conditioning and a seating area. There is a kitchen with a microwave and a fridge. Featuring a shower, private bathrooms also come with linen.

At Au Village de Menard you will find an airport shuttle, a garden and a terrace. Other facilities offered include a tour desk, luggage storage and a laundry.
An array of activities can be enjoyed on site or in the surroundings, including

A Casita

Located in Grand-Bourg, A Casita features free WiFi, a garden and outdoor pool. Le Gosier is 41 km from the property. Free private parking is available on site.

All units have a flat-screen TV. There is also a kitchenette, equipped with a microwave and toaster. A fridge and stovetop are also featured, as well as a coffee machine. Towels and bed linen are available.

Car hire is available at the property and the area is popular for diving. Sainte-Anne is 38 km from A Casita, while Saint-François is 40 km away. The nearest airport is Guadeloupe - Pôle Caraïbes Airport, 48 km from the property.

Villa Maria'Landa
This property is 6 minutes walk from the beach. Located in Capesterre, this air-conditioned villa features free WiFi and a terrace. Guests benefit from balcony and an outdoor pool. Free private parking is available on site.

The kitchen features a dishwasher, an oven and a microwave, as well as a coffee machine and a kettle. Towels and bed linen are available at Villa Maria'Landa. Other facilities at Villa Maria'Landa include a year-round outdoor pool.

Car hire is available at the property and the area is popular for snorkelling. Le Gosier is 45 km from Villa Maria'Landa, while Sainte-Anne is 41 km away. Guests can enjoy various activities in the surroundings, including windsurfing and diving. Guadeloupe - Pôle Caraïbes Airport is 53 km from the property.

This property also has one of the best-rated locations in Capesterre! Guests are happier about it compared to other properties in the area.

This property is also rated for the best value in Capesterre! Guests are getting more for their money when compared to other properties in this city.
We speak your language!
Villa Maria'Landa has been welcoming Booking.com guests since 30 Apr 2015.

La Suite de Kaz'hamac

Located in Grand-Bourg, 41 km from Le Gosier, La Suite de Kaz'hamac features a year-round outdoor pool and views of the sea. Free private parking is available on site.

You will find a coffee machine in the room. Rooms are fitted with a private bathroom. For your comfort, you will find free toiletries and a hairdryer. La Suite de Kaz'hamac features free WiFi throughout the property. There is access to a shared kitchenett and pic nic area, subject to availability.

Guadeloupe - Pôle Caraïbes Airport is 48 km from the property.

We speak your language!

Maison de vacances 100 moulins

Featuring air conditioning, Maison de vacances 100 moulins offers accommodation in Saint-Louis. Le Gosier is 39 km from the property. Free private parking is available on site.

All units feature a flat-screen TV. There is also a kitchen, equipped with an oven. A microwave and toaster are also available, as well as a coffee machine. Bed linen is offered.

Sainte-Anne is 34 km from Maison de vacances 100 moulins, while Saint-François is 33 km away. The nearest airport is Guadeloupe - Pôle Caraïbes Airport, 46 km from the property.

Maison de vacances 100 moulins has been welcoming Booking.com guests since 15 Jul 2017.

Les Palmes du Moulin

Les Palmes du Moulin is set in Saint-Louis, 1.7 km from Anse Bambou Beach and 32 km from Le Gosier. Free private parking is available on site.

The bungalows are equipped with flat-screen TV, air conditioning, and a bathroom with shower. The kitchens are fully equipped, and guests can relax on the terrace, in the hammock or chaise lounge. Sheets and towels are provided.

The hotel also offers car hire and guests can enjoy activities 2 km at the beach and the river Old Fort, where can it be practiced the canoe-kayak and pedal boat.

Sainte-Anne is 27 km from Les Palmes du Moulin, while Saint-François is 28 km away and are accesible by boat. Guadeloupe - Pôle Caraïbes Airport is 39 km from the property.

This property also has one of the best-rated locations in Saint-Louis! Guests are happier about it compared to other properties in the area.

Couples particularly like the location — they rated it 8.9 for a two-person trip.

You get good value for money here, according to couples who spent time at the property. They rate it 8.8.

We speak your language!

Les Palmes du Moulin has been welcoming Booking.com guests since 28 Apr 2016.

Kristal'Inn Cottage Caraibe

This property is 12 minutes walk from the beach. Set in Capesterre, this detached villa features a terrace and a garden. The air-conditioned unit is 45 km from Le Gosier. Free WiFi is available and free private parking is available on site.

There is a seating area and a kitchen equipped with a dishwasher. Towels and bed linen are provided at Kristal'Inn Cottage Caraibe.

Sainte-Anne is 41 km from Kristal'Inn Cottage Caraibe, while Saint-François is 41 km from the property. The nearest airport is Guadeloupe - Pôle Caraïbes Airport, 52 km from Kristal'Inn Cottage Caraibe.

We speak your language!

Villas Coccoloba & Jacaranda

Offering free WiFi and a year-round outdoor pool, Villas Coccoloba & Jacaranda is situated in Capesterre. Le Gosier is 45 km from the property. Free private parking is available on site.

The accommodation is air conditioned and comes with a flat-screen TV with satellite channels. Some units feature a seating area and/or terrace. There is also a kitchen, fitted with a dishwasher. An oven, a microwave and toaster are also available, as well as a coffee machine and a kettle. There is a private bathroom with a bath or shower and free toiletries in each unit. Bed linen is provided.

Villas Coccoloba & Jacaranda also includes a sun terrace. The property also offers grocery delivery and packed lunches.

You can engage in various activities, such as horse riding and snorkelling. Sainte-Anne is 41 km from Villas

Coccoloba & Jacaranda, while Saint-François is 41 km away. The nearest airport is Guadeloupe - Pôle Caraïbes Airport, 53 km from the property.

We speak your language!
Villas Coccoloba & Jacaranda has been welcoming Booking.com guests since 11 Jul 2016.

Fleur d'Hibiscus

Located 34 km from Le Gosier, Fleur d'Hibiscus offers pet-friendly accommodation in Saint-Louis. Guests benefit from terrace and a terrace. Free private parking is available on site.

The kitchen features an oven, a microwave and a toaster, as well as a coffee machine. Towels and bed linen are provided at Fleur d'Hibiscus.

Sainte-Anne is 31 km from Fleur d'Hibiscus, while Saint-François is 33 km away. You can engage in various activities, such as windsurfing, diving and fishing. The nearest airport is Guadeloupe - Pôle Caraïbes Airport, 42 km from Fleur d'Hibiscus.

We speak your language!

Sarl Le Touloulou

Set in Capesterre, 46 km from Le Gosier, Sarl Le Touloulou boasts a restaurant and free WiFi. The resort has a barbecue and views of the sea, and guests can enjoy a drink at the bar. Free private parking is available on site.

Each room at this resort is air conditioned and is fitted with a flat-screen TV. Enjoy a cup of coffee or tea from your terrace or balcony. Each room has a private bathroom.

Sainte-Anne is 42 km from Sarl Le Touloulou, while Saint-François is 42 km away. The nearest airport is Guadeloupe - Pôle Caraïbes Airport, 53 km from Sarl Le Touloulou.

Couples particularly like the location — they rated it 8.3 for a two-person trip.

Sarl Le Touloulou has been welcoming Booking.com guests since 20 Apr 2016.

Coco Beach Marie-Galante

This property is 12 minutes walk from the beach. Located beachfront in the Grand-Bourg area, Coco Beach Marie-Galante offers its guests free parking and Wi-Fi access. The boat station is 3 km away. Breakfast is offered.

The rooms and apartments have a modern décor and minimalistic-style, plus all have plenty of natural light. Apartments have an equipped kitchen, and all feature a private bathroom with shower.

Popular activities guests can practice while staying at Coco Beach Marie-Galante are cycling, diving and snorkelling and paddle boarding. A car hire can be arranged at the port or with the hotel directly upon request for a fee.

Marie-Galante Airport is 1.6 km away. The property is also 5 minutes' drive from Grand-Bourg city centre and 4.2 km from Centre Hospitalier de Marie Galante.

Couples particularly like the location — they rated it 8.5 for a two-person trip.

We speak your language!

Coco Beach Marie-Galante has been welcoming Booking.com guests since 12 Sept 2013.

Villa Pistaches

Offering a terrace and views of the garden, Villa Pistaches is located in Grand-Bourg in the Marie Galante Region, 40 km from Le Gosier. Free private parking is available on site.

Every room includes a TV. Each room is equipped with a private bathroom. Villa Pistaches features free WiFi throughout the property.

There is a 24-hour front desk at the property.

Sainte-Anne is 38 km from Villa Pistaches, while Saint-François is 41 km away. Guadeloupe - Pôle Caraïbes Airport is 48 km from the property.

Villa Pistaches has been welcoming Booking.com guests since 25 Apr 2017.

Au Village de Menard

This property is 18 minutes' walk from the beach. Featuring an outdoor pool and a restaurant open for dinner and for breakfast, Au Village de Menard it's located 2 km from the old fort from the beach, 5 km from Mays and 8 km from Saint Louis village. Free Wi Fi in public areas is available.

The rooms here will provide you with a TV, air conditioning and a seating area. There is a kitchen with a microwave and a fridge. Featuring a shower, private bathrooms also come with linen.

At Au Village de Menard you will find an airport shuttle, a garden and a terrace. Other facilities offered include a tour desk, luggage storage and a laundry.

An array of activities can be enjoyed on site or in the surroundings, including diving and canoeing.

Le Raizet Airport is 40 km away. The property offers free parking.

Couples particularly like the location — they rated it 8.5 for a two-person trip.

You get good value for money here, according to couples who spent time at the property. They rate it 8.1.

Au Village de Menard has been welcoming Booking.com guests since 26 Dec 2013.

La Kallina

Located on the small island of Marie Galante, La Kallina features an outdoor swimming pool and a garden. Free private parking is available and WiFi is provided at the reception desk.

La Kallina's air-conditioned studios and bungalows are self-contained and feature a closet, TV with cable channels and a private bathroom. Some of them have a private terrace and garden view.

A variety of restaurants and bars can be found within 1.5 km from the property. Activities in the vicinity of the property include hiking, surfing, kayaking and bicycling.

Capesterre is a 10 minutes' drive, while Grand Bourg can be reached within 5 minutes. Marie Galante Airport is 5 km from the property.

We speak your language!

La Kallina has been welcoming Booking.com guests since 28 Mar 2013.

Transportation

Transportation Options for Marie Galante
Sailing and driving are the main forms of transportation on Marie Galante

The largest of Guadeloupe's outer islands is Marie Galante, yet it remains a quiet tourist destination that attracts those looking for a more peaceful getaway. French in style, but wholly Caribbean at the same time, the unique blend allows this island to soar. Marie Galante is a popular day trip for those staying on the more tourist-driven islands in the chain, and both those staying for a few hours or a few days will need to know which options are available to them with regards to transportation.

Air Travel

If you're planning to fly to your vacation, your first stop will be in Pointe a Pitre at Le Raizet Airport (PTP). From there, you have the choice of hiring a charter to the smaller airport on Marie Galante, but most people choose to take the ferry, which you can read about below. Meanwhile, for more information about Marie Galante Air Travel, see air travel page in this book.

Sailing

Although the seas can sometimes be rough, Marie Galante is a great sailing destination thanks to its location in the Lower Antilles and the fact that it is an official port of entry for Guadeloupe. Sailors will find two marinas to choose from and several mooring sites. Learn all about sailing and boating on Marie Galante, read on Sailing & Boating in this book.

Cruises

If you're hoping to cruise to Marie Galante, be on the lookout for lines that sail to **Pointe a Pitre** on Grande Terre. When your ship docks here, you'll then be able to take the ferry over to the island, and many ships even offer excursions which will help to ensure their cruisers make it back to the boat on time.

Rental Cars

Renting a vehicle is a great way to get around Marie Galante, but not everyone wants to get around on four wheels. It is actually more common to rent a bicycle or a scooter. The local agencies offer both, so the choice is yours. Find out more about where you can rent from, how much it will cost, and even what driving conditions are like, read on Rental Cars page in ghis book.

Taxis

Taxis are available on Marie Galante, though they are not as plentiful as elsewhere in the country. Seasoned tourists would recommend that you keep this option in mind when necessary, but try and avoid them because the cost is so high. By reading our guide to Taxis on

Marie Galante page in this book, you'll learn more about the cost and where you can find a cab when in need.

Buses

There are two regular buses on Marie Galante every day. The first brings passengers to Grand Bourg from Capesterre, while the other travels from Grand Bourg to Saint-Louis. If you'd like to travel elsewhere on the island, you'll have to depend on mini-buses, which are harder to predict. The cost to ride is 2 Euros, which you pay upon arrival.

Ferries

Marie Galante connects via ferry with Pointe a Pitre several times a day. The trip take between 40 and 60 minutes depending on sailing conditions, and costs 33 Euros. A 45 minute ride is also available between Marie Galante and Terre de Haut, and during the height of tourist season a ferry ride opens up to and drom Les Saintes.

Marie Galante may not be one of the two main islands of Guadeloupe, but the transportation options available here are just as plentiful as elsewhere in the country. However you're hoping to get around, you shouldn't have any trouble making arrangements here.

Air Travel

How to Reach Marie Galante by Airplane?
It will take a ferry ride or a charter flight to complete your journey to Marie Galante

Once upon a time, you could fly all the way to Marie Galante via a small commercial flight, but these days that is a rarity. Now, most visitors will fly into the airport on Guadeloupe then take the ferry, or hire a charter to fly them the rest of the way to the island.

Pointe a Pitre Airport

Flights from the United States, Canada, London, and within the Caribbean make weekly, if not daily scheduled flights to the island of Grande Terre. The airport is located in Pointe a Pitre for which it is named, and is the largest airport in the country of the six that exist.

Flying to Marie Galante from the US

When you're looking for a flight to Marie Galante from the United States, American Airlines is the place to begin your search. They fly regularly out of Miami, and connections can be made from elsewhere in the country.

LE RAIZET AIRPORT U.S. FLIGHTS		
To/From	Airport Code	Airlines
Baltimore, MD, USA	BWI	Norwegian
Miami, FL, USA	MIA	Air France, American Airlines

Flying to Marie Galante from Canada

Air Canada offers direct flights to Guadeloupe from Montreal, through you'll be able to connect through Miami if you need to fly from Toronto or another major airport in the country.

LE RAIZET AIRPORT CANADIAN FLIGHTS		
To/From	Airport Code	Airlines
Montreal, Canada	YUL	Air Canada

Flying to Marie Galante from Europe

The London Heathrow Airport provides your sole direct connection from Europe with **Air** France on a regular basis. Most people traveling from Europe connect here, but it is also possible to fly to a large airport within the Caribbean and continue to the island from there.

Flying to Marie Galante from the Caribbean

For many, it will be easier to book a flight to another island in the Caribbean such as Antigua or the Dominican Republic, then fly with a regional carrier like LIAT and Winair.

LE RAIZET AIRPORT CARIBBEAN FLIGHTS		
To/From	Airport Code	Airlines
Antigua, Antigua and Barbuda	ANU	LIAT
Dominica	DOM	Air Antilles Express, LIAT, Winair
Dominican Republic	SDQ	Air Antilles Express, Air Caraibes, Air France
Grand Case, The island of St. Martin and Sint Maarten	SFG	Air Antilles Express, Air Caraibes
Gustavia, St. Barthelemy	SBH	Air Antilles Express
Isla Verde, Puerto Rico	SJU	Seaborne Airlines
Martinique	FDF	Air Antilles Express, Air Caraibes, Air France
Simpson Bay, The island of St. Martin and Sint Maarten	SXM	Air Antilles Express

It may take a bit of work to plan to travel to Marie Galante, but just a few extra steps is all you need and you'll be on your way to the quiet island getaway of your dreams.

Rental Cars

Marie Galante Rental Cars
Get out and explore with a rental car on Marie Galante

For hands-on exploring at your own pace, consider renting a car for your stay on Marie Galante. Prices are low and appear to be even more affordable when you consider the high cost of taking a taxi, restrictions are limited, and conditions are good. These three things make renting a car the recommended course of action.

Renting a Car

Renting a car on Marie Galante is a fairly easy process. You'll need a valid driver's license from your country of origin and the means to pay. Otherwise, other restrictions are entirely up to your rental agency. You'll find a variety of vehicles, including scooters and bicycles to be available for rent here. If you plan on exploring the entire island, a car or sports utility vehicle is recommended; however, if you plan to stick near your accommodations, a might be the perfect fit for you.

Hertz is the one rental service we have information on. You can give them a call at (059) 097-5980, or find them in the northeastern part of Marie-Galante.

The Cost of Renting a Car
The cost of renting a vehicle will vary by season and by the type of vehicle you rent, but in general, you can expect to spend no less than $32 and no higher than $100(USD). This does not include the optional insurance, which is recommended, and keep in mind

that you may be expended to pay a deposit. Contact the rental agency to find out for sure.

Driving on Marie Galante
The generally flat terrain makes driving on Marie Galante fairly easy to manage, especially for those who are considering getting around on two wheels. Do keep in mind that whether you choose a bicycle or a motor bike, you'll be required by law to wear a helmet. Traffic moves on the right side of the road like in the United States. Overall, it can be said that the road conditions here are good, though the lack of signs can make getting lost easy if you aren't paying close attention at all times.

In the end, you'll have to go with the form of transportation that feels right to you, but know that when it comes to getting around Marie Galante, most will recommend renting a car.

Sailing & Boating

Sailing and Boating Near Marie Galante
Marie Galante is a top sailing destination in Guadeloupe

South of the two main islands of Guadeloupe is Marie Galante, a much quieter destination that tends to appeal to sailors for exactly that reason. The more laid back atmosphere is exactly what someone who has been at sea for a few days is looking for, and it helps that this island is an official port of entry.

If you're considering the option of a charter boat, you can reserve one from the following agencies:

CHARTER AND RENTAL SERVICES		
Name	Phone	Location
Clair de Vent	(069) 048-5138	20 Résidence Club Marine - Ste. Anne
Excursion Guadeloupe	(069) 074-8057	93 Impasse Du Poisson Chirurgien - Ste. Anne
TAO Charter	(059) 088-0517	23 Poirier de Gissac - Ste. Anne

Docking

First things first. If you have any questions as you sail to Marie Galante, you'd do well to contact the Central Office of Maritime Security in the Antilles over VHF Channel 16. Then, as you sail in to port, have your quarantine flag flying to let officials know that you've not yet been granted clearance. Only the captain will meet with officials as the others wait behind, presenting a crew list and passports for each person aboard, a list of the ship's stores, clearance papers from your last port of call, and an original copy of the boat's registration. If this is all in order, you should have no problem officially obtaining entry and being granted permission to cruise throughout the island.

If you're planning to stay on the island long term, you'll find two great marinas where you can dock, but there are also a few mooring locations to consider as well.

Considering sailing to Marie Galante using your own boat, or a charter from another location? This next chart lists potential docking spots.

MARINAS	
Name	Location
Grand Bourg Port Marina	Grand-Bourg
Marie Galante Marina	Marie-Galante

Sailing is a great way to get to Marie Galate, as it is also a pleasurable experience for just a few hours of fun. If you've got the skills to sail yourself, many who have made the journey before would recommend it.

Taxis

Marie Galante Taxis
Call when you need a taxi on Marie Galante
As the largest island outside of mainland Guadeloupe, there is a lot of ground to cover on Marie Galante.

Taxis are available, but using them as your main source of transportation will cost you a pretty penny, so most tourists keep them in mind in case of emergency rather than making them their regular way to get around.

Taxi Companies

While taxis are available throughout the island, especially in the main towns of Grand-Bourg, Saint-Louis, and Capesterre, they can be extremely hard to come by. If you do see one on the street it will be in the form of a minivan, and you'll have a good chance of encountering one at the ferry terminal. Otherwise, your best chance at getting a private ride is to call the service directly. Most operators speak French, so if this isn't a language you are fluent in ask someone at your accommodations to place the call and arrange this form of transportation for you.

MTL Taxis is the only taxi service for which we have detailed info. You can contact them at (069) 083-1109; they're located in the eastern part of Marie-Galante.

Rates, Fares, and Fees

There is no getting around it; taking a taxi on Marie Galante is the most expensive way to travel. It is about 1 Euro per minute, which comes out to about $1.36(USD) per minute. Traffic will affect the price in this case, so a ride from your accommodations to the beach can be slightly different than the ride back. Drivers are willing to negotiate the fare, though the price is technically set by the government, so you may be able to save money if you promise to always use a certain driver when you're in need of a ride. Make room for gratuities in your budget as well.

If you don't feel comfortable driving in a foreign country, taxis will be your most reliable way of getting around, but it comes at a cost. If you are willing to pay, there is nothing to recommend against take a taxi on Marie Galante.

Guide to Marie Galante

How to Get There

Airport

Marie Galante airport is located in the south of the island between Grand Bourg and Capesterre.

Airlines From The Uk

Air France (0845 084 5111; www.airfrance.com) flies from London Heathrow to Pointe-à-Pitre via Paris. From Pointe-à-Pitre, Air Guadeloupe (00 590 82 47 00) flies to Marie Galante three times a day; journey time is 15 minutes. It is not always possible to get from Pointe-à-Pitre to Marie Galante in the same day if you are coming from overseas.

By Boat

Boats leave two or three times a day from La Darse,

the port in Pointe-à-Pitre, to Saint Louis and Grand Bourg. Brudey Frères (00 590 90 04 48) and L'Express des Iles (00 590 83 12 45) are two of the operators. The journey costs about FF170 and takes 45 minutes; it can be rough.

Where to stay

L'auberge De L'arbre A Pain
Grand Bourg(00 590 97 73 69)

Clean with restaurant, air conditioning and hot water, but no other frills.

Hotel Cohoba
Grand Bourg(00 590 97 50 50)

Marie Galante's only 'proper' hotel. Three-star with 100 rooms, a swimming pool, all mod cons but singularly without charm. Credit cards accepted except American Express.

Le Salut

Saint Louis(00 590 97 02 67)

A small modest hotel; there is no hot water or air conditioning, but staff can provide meals.

Chez Hajo
Capesterre(00 590 97 32 76)

A very pretty, quiet and rather chic French-run place on the sea. No hot water or air conditioning.

Village De Menard
Vieux-Fort(00 590 97 09 45)

Pretty little cottages with air conditioning, close to lovely Vieux Fort but quite cut off.

Matamin
Vieux-Fort

Five pretty solar-powered wooden bungalows and one kitchen bungalow for communal (vegetarian-only) use.

Anchorage Hotel St John
Near La Darse, Pointe-à-Pitre, Guadeloupe(00 590 82 51 57)

If you have to stay in Guadeloupe, try the Anchorage Hôtel St John, a perfectly good modern hotel.

When to Go

Marie Galante has a warm climate with temperatures averaging 25ºC. It is the perfect winter sun escape (Dec to Feb) with sun guaranteed and rainfall usually limited to short, thundery showers.

Tourist Info

There is a Bureau Touristique de Marie-Galante (00 590 97 77 48) on the island.

Travel Tips

Very few people speak anything other than French, but they are usually prepared to be helpful even if your French is limited.

Take Euros or US dollars (the latter is the only foreign currency you can change). The commission on changing US-dollar traveller's cheques is very steep and it is difficult to find anywhere that will do it at all. There are some ATMs. Visa is far more widely accepted than any other card but most places take cash only.

In hotels, hot water is the exception rather than the rule, unless you are staying somewhere smart.

You will need mosquito coils, but you can buy them on the island.

Topless bathing is permitted, but be circumspect.

At the airport, try to get hold of a free copy of *Ti Gourmet*, an annual list of hotels and restaurants.

Travel Information

Visas: Visas are not required of citizens of the US, Canada or the European Union. Citizens of the EU need an official identity card, passport or valid French carte de séjour. Citizens of most other foreign countries, including Australia, need a valid passport and visa for

France. All visitors officially require a return or onward ticket.

Public holidays: New Year's Day; Easter Holidays - Ash Wednesday, Good Friday, Easter Sunday, Easter Monday; Labour Day; Victory Day (8 May); Ascension Thursday; Pentecost Monday; Slavery Abolition Day (27 May); Bastille Day (14 July); Schoelcher Day (21 July 21); Assumption Day; All Saints' Day; Armistice Day; Christmas Day.

Good buys: Sugar, bananas and rum.

Local dishes: Varied, with far-off origins, Creole cooking takes advantage of the resources of the sea and the creativity of the inhabitants.

Good reading: Saint-John Perse, the pseudonym of poet Alexis Léger born in Guadeloupe in 1887, won the Nobel Prize for Literature in 1960. One of his many noted works is Anabase, which was translated into

English by TS Eliot. The leading contemporary novelist in the French West Indies is Guadeloupe native Maryse Condé. Try her epic The Tree of Life, which tells the story of a Guadeloupean family, or Crossing the Mangrove, a pleasant tale about relationships.

Sightseeing and things to do

Marie Galante is a small, virtually round island about 25km from the Guadeloupe mainland. It was 'discovered' by Columbus in 1493, on his second voyage to the Antilles. He named the island after the admiral's flagship, the *Marigalante*. Its main agriculture is the cultivation of sugar cane and its only industry the manufacture of strong rum, usually 59 per cent proof (it used to be 65 per cent). Marie Galantine rum is said to be the best in the world. The island has three functioning distilleries, and a number of picturesque ruins that testify to its sugarcane past.

Ruins

The best-known of these ruins is the late 18th-century Château Murat, which lies just outside the island's capital, Grand-Bourg, on the road to Capesterre. The château is an impressive reminder of just how rich Marie Galante must once have been. A large, seriously grand house, now gutted inside, it stands at the top of a gentle incline, commanding a magnificent view of the sea. Nearby lie the ruins of the sugar factory and a windmill. There were once 100 such windmills on Marie Galante, some 70 of these are still standing. The Habitation Roussel (habitation means 'estate house') on the road to Saint Louis is much smaller, but pretty and very picturesque.

Grand bourg

There are two ports on the island: the capital, Grand Bourg, and Saint Louis. Although Grand Bourg is just another dusty little Caribbean town, it is home to the pretty Notre Dame de Marie Galante church. Built in

1827, it has a splendid vaulted wooden ceiling painted a bright sky-blue and an elaborate marble altar with a bas-relief of the Last Supper.

Beaches

Marie Galante has beautiful, white-sand beaches and wonderful, clear waters which it shares with Guadeloupe (the Carib name for Guadeloupe was Karukera which meant 'Island of Beautiful Waters'). On the west coast, lovely beaches can be found at Anse Canot, Moustique, Folle Anse and Trois Ilets. The beach at Vieux Fort (see above), north of Saint Louis, offers picnic accommodations while the beach at Grand Bourg is protected by a coral reef that makes its shallow waters ideal for children. On the east coast, Petite Anse, Les Galets and Anse Feuillard all offer great beaches. The sensational Plage de la Feuillère at Capesterre is also protected by a coral reef while Anse Taliseronde offers incredible snorkelling.

5 Things to do in Marie-Galante, Guadeloupe

The island Marie-Galante forms part of the Guadeloupe archipelago, a French Caribbean overseas department. The island has about 12,000 inhabitants and the capital is Grand Bourg. Marie-Galante offers more than only white sandy beaches. Did you know there were more than 100 windmills spread across the island? It is also called the island of sugar. Ideal for day trips from Basse-Terre or Grande-Terre, but Marie-Galante deserves more than that. I'll tell you about 5 things to do in Marie-Galante!

Marie-Galante is easily reached by ferry in about 45 minutes from Guadeloupe's capital Pointe-a-Pitre. The ferry goes to both Grand Bourg and Saint-Louis. It's best to explore Marie-Galante by scooter or by car. The infrastructure on the island is in very good condition. Due to the low population density, it is very calm, there are only 12,000 inhabitants! When you're here you're not in a hurry, which makes it ideal to relax and unwind!

Relaxing on the beach

Plage de la Feuillère, the absolute paradise for beach lovers, like myself! An idyllic white sandy beach, waving palm trees and a babbling Caribbean Sea overlooking neighboring island Dominica. A handful of beach bars are hidden between the palm trees. Another beautiful beach in Marie-Galante is Plage à Saint Louis. Something elongated and somewhat more narrow with palms and tropical scrub. A beautiful turquoise colored Caribbean Sea with scenic view on Basse-Terre, the 'mainland' of Guadeloupe. Bring drinks yourself, because there are no beach bars.

Rum tasting

Rum lovers pay attention: one of the world's best best rum is distilled in Marie-Galante. As a matter of fact on this small island there are still three operating distilleries, 'Distillerie Poisson', 'Distillerie Bielle', and 'Habitation Bellevue'. The best thing is you can visit them all. They welcome you warmly and you can taste the many varieties of rum...for free!

Spotting windmills
Marie-Galante used to be a big sugar cane producer. Spread across the island you will find numerous ancient ruins of windmills. Some still in good condition, others are overgrown by nature. Some of then are still in use, at the rum distilleries for example.

Visit Grand Bourg
The capital of the island. Despite the fact it looks like a typical Caribbean town, there are certainly some old gems to be found. Including a church from 1827, Notre Dame de Marie Galante, worth a visit. In addition, there are several nice restaurants to be found as well. For example, enjoy dining at Maria Galanda!

Having fun and sightseeing while driving around

The island is as flat as a pancake, as a result making it easy to ride. Explore the island by rental car or scooter. On your way you'll encounter all kinds of (historical) beauties, such as the Château Murat, an old 1883 plantation house with beautiful sea views and used to be the largest sugar cane plantation of Guadeloupe. Or Habitation Roussel, an old but well-maintained 17th century plantation house on the road to Saint Louis. All the way north you'll find Guele Grand Gouffre, a kind of naturally bridged impressive rock, beautiful with the turquoise crawling sea.

Shopping

Travelers should be able to find most of the things they need in the interesting shops of Grand-Bourg, Saint-Louis or Capesterre. Marie-Galante offers a growing number of boutiques for tourists, featuring jewelry, pottery, sculpture, embroidery, lace and other textiles. Traditional dolls and masks, as well as confections and locally-produced coconut and manioc flour are also available. Of course, fine rums and delicious fruit punches can be found everywhere. The open air markets in Grand-Bourg and Saint-Louis offer a more traditional shopping experience.

Most shops in Marie-Galante are open Monday - Friday from 9:00 to 13:00, then close for a long lunch, reopening at 15:00 or 16:00 for several more hours. Some shops are also open on Saturday mornings. Prices are in Euros and credit cards are widely accepted.

Restaurant

Restaurant Options on Marie Galante
There is not an overabundance of dining options on Marie Galante, but what you will find is a lot of high

quality establishments serving French, Creole, and Caribbean fare. Whether you stop into a cafe for a quick bite, or sit down to dinner with a view of the sea, you'll be treated to a meal that will be hard to forget and service that makes you feel like royalty.

Caribbean and Local

Diners will find a handful of opportunities to enjoy trying local flavors throughout their time on Marie Galante. Creole and Caribbean dishes are a couple of the selections you'll find in the area. Remember to click on the links to read further info.

Le Touloulou is a local bar and grill located in southeastern Marie Galante. This restaurant specializes in things that are filling but great for a day at the beach, like fish and kebabs. If you'd like to call ahead of time, you can do so at (059) 097-3263.

A good place you could visit is Manman'dlo La Sirene. Manman'dlo translates to mermaid in English, which is a fun name for a restaurant set by the pool. You'll dine in a relaxed outdoor setting and be treated to world cuisine made fresh to your order. They're located on Route du littoral.

Le Maria-Galanda: Made with fresh produce from local farmers and seafood brought in by local fishermen, the menu at this restaurant is always a treat. You'll find them at 30 rue du Docteur Etzol.

View more information on similar types of eateries within Marie Galante by taking a look at the chart down below.

CARIBBEAN AND LOCAL RESTAURANTS ON MARIE GALANTE			
Name	Location	Type	Phone Number
Aux Plaisirs des Marins	0.6 mi. North of Central Saint Louis	Creole	(059) 097-0811

La Playa	5.2 mi. East of Central Grand-Bourg	Caribbean	(059) 093-6610
Le Maria-Galanda	0.0 mi. South West of Central Saint Louis	Creole	(059) 097-5056
Le Touloulou	5.3 mi. East of Central Grand-Bourg	Creole	(059) 097-3263
Manman'dlo La Sirene	5.0 mi. East of Central Grand-Bourg	Caribbean	(059) 097-5743

European and Asian

Le Murato is a laid-back restaurant found in Grand-Bourg, Marie Galante. Although closed on Sundays, you can grab dinner from 5:30 to 11:00 p.m. throughout the rest of the week. You can contact them at (059) 046-0651.

EUROPEAN AND ASIAN RESTAURANTS ON MARIE GALANTE				
Name	Location	Island	Type	Phone Number

| Le Murato | Grand-Bourg, Southwestern part of Marie Galante | Marie-Galante | Italian | (059) 046-0651 |

Le Touloulou

Eat with your feet in the sand when you dine at the relaxed and even fun Le Touloulou. It is the perfect spot to grab a bite during your day on the beach.

Food

This restaurant specializes in things that are filling but great for a day at the beach, like fish and kebabs.

Le Touloulou is a bar and grill where they proudly serve their take on Creole cuisine. The style of the restaurant and its dishes is considered by most to be very casual. When is this restaurant option on the table? They're open during both dinner and lunch, so make time to stop by; you could find a new favorite food.

Ambiance

Brightly decorated, this is a true beach grill setting complete with outdoor seating and views of the sea.

Location

This restaurant is on the beach, located on the island of Marie-Galante, 5.3 miles East of Grand-Bourg. Le Touloulou is a nice choice for those lodging in the area. Local customers and vacationers who are checking out Pointe A Pitre might also consider dining here, as it's 31.7 miles to the southeast of the city.

One benefit of stopping or staying in the area near this location is Petite-Anse, a nearby beach, where tired travelers can recharge on the warm sand.

Nearby Restaurants
For diners seeking out a local restaurant with some similar kinds of food and/or comparable prices, there are at least a couple of nearby places to pick from, including La Playa.

But then again, if you're in the mood for a change of pace, there is a pretty good selection of restaurant options in the area that serve other kinds of cooking styles and menu items. For instance, you can try Caribbean fare at Manman'dlo La Sirene, which is a half mile away.

Most people spend around $20(USD) per person when they dine here.

Contact Info

Location: Marie-Galante
Phone: (059) 097-3263

Website: http://www.letouloulou.com/
Email: touloulou@wanadoo.fr

Manman'dlo La Sirene

Manman'dlo translates to mermaid in English, which is a fun name for a restaurant set by the pool. You'll dine in a relaxed outdoor setting and be treated to world cuisine made fresh to your order.

Food

Fresh, organic offerings are used as often as possible to create every dish on the menu.

Manman'dlo La Sirene is a bar and grill where they proudly serve their take on Caribbean cuisine. Most guests consider the level of formality and service here to be informal. This eatery is open for both breakfast and dinner, so make time to stop by; you could find a new favorite food.

Location

This restaurant is part of La Rose du Brésil, which is found on the island of Marie-Galante, 5.0 miles east of Grand-Bourg; it's 31.5 miles to the southeast of Pointe A Pitre.

Travelers wanting to merge their visit to the restaurant with some nice sightseeing possibilities should think about heading to Rhum Belle Distillery, which is situated 2.8 miles to the north-northwest.

Something else to try besides the food the area near this restaurant is Petite-Anse, a beach where you could either work up your appetite, or wind down after a meal.

Nearby Restaurants
If you and your party are looking for another nearby restaurant where you can get some Caribbean food, you might enjoy La Playa.

Then of course, if you're in the mood for a change of pace, there is a pretty good selection of dining establishments nearby that offer other kinds of foods and flavors. For instance, you can also try Creole cuisine at Le Touloulou, which is located right on the beach.

Hours and Other Info
Food is included as part of the extra all-inclusive plan at this hotel.

Breakfast is served from 7:30 to 9:0 a.m. while dinner begins at 7:00 p.m.

Contact Info

Location: Route du littoral, Marie-Galante
Phone: (059) 097-5743
Website: http://www.hotel-mariegalante.com/

Le Maria-Galanda

Set on a rustic patio surrounded by greenery, Le Maria-Galanda is known for its unique surroundings, locally harvested food, and friendly, urgent staff.

Food

Made with fresh produce from local farmers and seafood brought in by local fishermen, the menu at this restaurant is always a treat.

Le Maria-Galanda is a bistro where they proudly serve their take on Creole cuisine. Most guests consider the level of formality and service here to be informal. When's the best time to come? They're open for dinner only, so don't miss their brief service.

Ambiance

When you eat at Le Maria-Galanda, you're dining out on a patio surrounded by palm trees, jasmine, orchids, and papyrus, and in the waters nearby there are three turtles always popping up for a visit. Although the setting is casual, it is somehow magical as well.

Location

Le Maria-Galanda is located in Saint Louis, a town on Marie-Galante; it's 24 miles (39 kilometers) to the southeast of Pointe A Pitre.

One benefit of stopping or staying in this neighborhood is Anse de Mays, a nearby beach, where tired travelers can recharge on the warm sand.

Nearby Restaurants
If you and your group are looking for another nearby restaurant that serves Creole fare, consider visiting Le Touloulou.

Of course, if you're in the mood for a change of pace, there is a pretty good selection of dining possibilities nearby that feature other kinds of menu items and cuisine styles. For instance, you might also consider trying Italian eats at Le Murato, which is five miles south.

Hours and Other Info
Meals generally cost around $20(USD) per guest.

Closed on Thursday, dinner is served from 7:00 to 10:00 p.m. throughout the rest of the week.

Contact Info

Location: 30 rue du Docteur Etzol, Saint Louis, Marie-Galante

Phone: (059) 097-5056
Website: https://www.facebook.com/lemariagalanda

Le Murato

Your favorite family-friendly pizzeria, Le Murato is a great spot to stop and share a pie and enjoy a good time in a relaxed atmosphere.

Food
Le Murato is a popular carry out restaurant that happens to specialize in Italian cuisine. As far as service and setting, you can expect the formality to be very casual. When is this restaurant option on the table? They're open during both dinner and lunch, so make time to try it.

Ambiance
Dining takes place out on a wooden patio that is covered by open air so the sun can shine in and the breeze can keep things cool. The decor is contemporary and comfortable, mixing lounge and bistro style in a casual atmosphere.

Location
Positioned in the heart of Grand-Bourg. Le Murato is an inviting choice for those staying in the region. Local residents and travelers who are checking out Basse Terre might also think about dining here, since it is 28 miles (45 kilometers) to the east-southeast of the city.

This part of Marie-Galante has many attractions and landmarks, making it a vivacious town. Two of the closest visitor favorites from this particular dining option include Jardin de l'Habitation Murat and Distillerie Poisson, both of which are only a short distance from Le Murato.

Something else to see during your time in the area near this location is Plage de Folle Anse, which is nearby beach where the entire family can relax.

Nearby Restaurants
Being able to choose from among several different restaurants can make a great day even better during a relaxing holiday. This section of Marie-Galante is home to a fair selection of restaurants, serving different types of culinary offerings. For more overall flavors, enjoy small portions at Le Murato, then also make plans to dine on the Creole cuisine at Le Maria-Galanda, which is five miles away.

Hours and Other Info
Although closed on Sundays, you can grab dinner from 5:30 to 11:00 p.m. throughout the rest of the week.

Contact Info

Location: Grand-Bourg, Marie-Galante
Phone: (059) 046-0651

Activities

Activities on Marie Galante

small island off the coast of Guadeloupe, Marie Galante has that deserted isle feel that many tourists crave when they visit the Caribbean. Those who travel here are able to connect with nature, and the main activity, aside from relaxing on the beach, is sightseeing.

Diving

Marie Galante Diving

There are dive operators in the area. Visit "Diving" page dedicated to diving in this area if you're seeking more specifics.

Shopping

Shopping in Guadeloupe

For information concerning opportunities for shopping on Marie Galante, see Shopping page in this book.

Sightseeing

Sightseeing is another great way to spend some of your time on Marie Galante. Among other sights, the area has a historic site and some distilleries. Those visitors who enjoy being outside might enjoy visiting the botanical gardens and other natural attractions. To learn more about area sightseeing attractions, on Attraction page in this book.

Snorkeling

If exploring a watery world sounds fun there's good news -- you can easily find places to do so in the waters surrounding Marie Galante. To read our guide to local snorkeling opportunities, see Snorkeling page in his book.

Other Activities

Details concerning one other option is shown below.

OTHER ACTIVITIES ON MARIE GALANTE				
Name	Type	Phone	Location	Island
Aichi Fun Jet Skis	Jet Ski Rental Service	(069) 065-3372	Saint Louis, Western part of Marie Galante	Marie-Galante

Diving

Scuba Diving Near Marie Galante

For such a small island, Marie Galante offers a truly amazing array of coral reefs just off shore. It's no wonder that many of the people come here for the diving -- or decide to give it a try, if they've never gone diving before.

You'll find dive services to choose from.

Dive Operators

If you're ready to dive, you can check with Ti'bulles Dive Center. A relatively new dive center, owners

Muriel and Stephane lived on a sailboat for 7 years before settling on Marie Galante. They are now very happy to share their passion for the sea with fellow divers. They are located in southwestern Marie Galante.

Another good option is Man'balaou Club de Plongee. With 20 years of diving experience in the charming Marie Galante Bay area, Man'balaou Club de Plongee is an eco-friendly diving service that provides a pleasant atmosphere and several activities for all ages. You can reach them at (059) 097-7524.

A few details regarding area dive operators can be seen in this chart:

DIVE OPERATORS NEAR MARIE GALANTE		
Name	Phone	Location
Man'balaou Club de Plongee	(059) 097-7524	0.0 mi. South West of Central Saint Louis

| Ti'bulles Dive Center | (059) 097-5490 | 0.6 mi. Southeast of Central Grand-Bourg |

Ti'bulles Dive Center

A relatively new dive center, owners Muriel and Stephane lived on a sailboat for 7 years before settling on Marie Galante. They are now very happy to share their passion for the sea with fellow divers.

Offerings and Cost

Your safety and pleasure are ensured at Ti'bulles regardless of your skill level. Activities offered include beach tours of Marie Galante, baptisms, first dives, snorkeling, wreck sites, and multilevel exploration dives. Complimentary drinks are available after your time on the water.

Baptisms range from $42-50. Exploration dive package and training course rates vary; see their website for additional details.

Location and Contact Information

Positioned on the southwestern side of the island of Marie-Galante, in the vicinity of Grand-Bourg, Ti'bulles Dive Center will be happy to serve local customers and travelers who would enjoy diving during their vacation on this part of the island or nearby. It's east-southeast of Basse Terre.

Location: Rue Beaurenom, Marie-Galante
Phone: (059) 097-5490
Website: http://www.tibulles-plongee.com/

Man'balaou Club de Plongee

With 20 years of diving experience in the charming Marie Galante Bay area, Man'balaou Club de Plongee is an eco-friendly diving service that provides a pleasant atmosphere and several activities for all ages.

Cost and Offerings

All equipment is provided for your convenience. Multilevel training courses, explorations, and trips to popular dive sites are arranged for you according to experience and skill level. There are more than six beautiful dive sites that the center frequents.

Single tank dives start at $45(USD); night dives are $55. 10 dive packages are available starting at $388. Training course prices vary by level and quantity of dives, but they start at $200. Prices do not exceed $500 for the most advanced course with a 10 dive package included.

What to Expect

Children aged 8 and older are welcome to dive at Man'balaou Club de Plongee.

For more information about diving in the Caribbean, including useful suggestions and tips for both experienced divers and newcomers to the sport, read our comprehensive guide to **scuba diving** in the Caribbean.

Location and Contact Information

Man'balaou Club de Plongee is located near the center of Saint Louis, a town on Marie-Galante; it is to the southeast of Pointe A Pitre.

Location: Avenue des Caraïbes, Saint Louis, Marie-Galante

Phone: (059) 097-7524

Secondary Phone: (059) 097-7524

Website: http://plongee-marie-galante.com/

Email: manbalaou@plongee-marie-galante.com

Snorkeling

Snorkeling Around Marie Galante

The waters off the shores of Marie Galante include world-class coral reefs that can be enjoyed by both experienced and inexperienced snorkelers. You'll discover an amazing profusion of tropical fish, lobsters and other undersea creatures.

Snorkeling Services

If you're looking for someone that offers snorkel rentals, excursions, or similar services, you might want to contact Ti'bulles Snorkeling. Although primarily a dive center, the owners, Muriel and Stephane, also welcome snorkelers to experience the beautiful coral reefs off the shores of Marie Galante. You can arrange for a private snorkeling tour that includes visits to remote beaches and superb snorkeling sites. They are located in the southwestern part of Marie Galante.

The following table enables you to learn information regarding two firms that provide services of interest to snorkelers.

SNORKELING SERVICES ON MARIE GALANTE		
Name	Phone	Location

Man'balaou Club de Plongee	(059) 097-7524	0.0 mi. South West of Central Saint Louis
Ti'bulles Snorkeling	(059) 097-5490	0.6 mi. Southeast of Central Grand-Bourg

To learn more concerning snorkeling, including tips and suggestions for both "old pros" and beginners, read this exhaustive guide to snorkeling in the Caribbean.

Attractions

Attractions on Marie Galante

Marie Galante has a rural appeal that allows its guests to keep things simple. Most visitors spend their days on the beaches, or taking advantage of a number of local hiking trails, but you can also spend some time learning about how this island has flourished over the years by checking out local museums and landmarks that pay particular focus to agricultural advances.

Beaches

You will find an abundance of beaches to visit on the island. You can click on each beach name for a detailed article concerning that particular stretch of sand.

Anse Canot: In addition, all of the regular beach activities, visitors to Anse Canot can enjoy a variety of water sports off the coast of Anse Canot. There are no facilities, however, so be sure to bring your own supplies.

Another place for beach-goers to consider is Plage de Folle Anse. When on the island of Marie Galante, simply follow the coastal road D-206. Plage de Folle Anse is located between Anse La Frais and Ansa Ballet.

Petite-Anse: Soak up some sun on the beach or head out to deeper waters for a magnificent scuba diving excursion. Scuba trips depart from the shores three times each day.

These examples are just some of the available choices. Read on Beach page dedicated to beaches for Marie Galante.

Museums

If you enjoy expanding your knowledge of unfamiliar places and cultures, you should consider visiting a museum while on vacation on Marie Galante.

One popular destination is Ecomussee de Marie Galante. It is found in southern Marie Galante. Learn everything you need to know about one of the quieter islands in Guadeloupe, Marie Galante, at this cultural and history museum.

The chart just below lists some details regarding a museum you might enjoy on Marie Galante.

MUSEUMS ON MARIE GALANTE			
Name	Phone	Location	Island
Ecomussee de	(059)	1.0 mi. East-Southeast	Marie-

| Marie Galante | 097-4868 | of Central Grand-Bourg | Galante |

Historical Sites

In case you enjoy exploring the historical roots of a foreign country, you should consider visiting a historical site during your stay.

HISTORIC SITES ON MARIE GALANTE				
Name	Type	Phone	Location	Island
Delices de Siblet Sugar Factory	Historical Site	(059) 097-0287	0.6 mi. North of Central Grand-Bourg	Marie-Galante

Miscellaneous Landmarks

Guests can enjoy some other interesting sites on the island.

The table directly below provides you with more information on the other kinds of attractions of interest to visitors.

MISCELLANEOUS LANDMARKS ON MARIE GALANTE		
Name	Type	Location
Distillerie Poisson	Distillery	0.5 mi. North-Northeast of Central Grand-Bourg
Rhum Belle Distillery	Distillery	Central Marie Galante

Botanical Gardens

Vacationers can spend some time in one of the botanical gardens on Marie Galante.

If you'd like to see some beautiful tropical vegetation, you might want to visit Jardin de Buckingham, which is located within Marie Galante. Discover the island's tradition of a garden hike with the Vinbatamarin family as you explore these beautiful and flourishing grounds.

The gardens worth considering are shown right below.

GARDENS ON MARIE GALANTE

Name	Type	Location
Jardin de Buckingham	Botanical Garden	0.7 mi. North-Northeast of Central Grand-Bourg
Jardin de l'Habitation Murat	Botanical Garden	0.1 mi. South of Central Grand-Bourg

Despite being the largest of Guadeloupe's outer islands, Marie Galante has small town feel. You can play off this and keep your sightseeing at a minimal, or go for it and squeeze them all in.

Museum

Ecomusee de Marie Galante (Grand Bourg)
Beautiful grounds and nice museum: First of all, it's free. Second of all, the grounds and main building are beautiful and the view of the ocean from the main building is spectacular. It's definitely worth an hour or so to walk around and see the displays in the museum. There are two signs on the grounds that give some of

the history of the old plantation in English. All the signs inside the main house are in French but there are a lot of photos so it's easy to figure out what things are. Highly recommended!

Beautiful location, nice gardens and well maintained site, worth a quick stop: The main house from this former sugar/rum plantation along some of the outbuildings and well-maintained gardens is a nice stop; and there are several kiosks in both French and English which provide information about the site. But, overall there isn't much here and this was a far cry from the level of information that we received in a similar plantation site in La Moule (the Zevallos House)

Beaches

Beaches on Marie Galante

There are about 10 beaches on the island of Marie Galante, and all are known for their clear waters and deserted sands. It is easy to feel as though you are the only person to have ever discovered the shores because you'll rarely encounter another person while you frolic in the sand. The best part about these beaches is that a coral reef system just off the coast keeps the waters calm enough that families find it easy to relax here.

Pick Your Ideal Beach
You will find an abundance of beaches to consider on the island. Just click on the name of each beach to read a detailed article concerning that section of the coast.

Plage de Folle Anse
If you want to snorkel, a beach where that is an option is Petite-Anse. Soak up some sun on the beach or head out to deeper waters for a magnificent scuba diving excursion. Scuba trips depart from the shores three times each day.

A second alternative that beach-goers can consider is Anse de l'Eglise. Enjoy canoeing in the fresh water alongside the beach or hike through the mangrove swamp. Anse de l'Eglise is a great place for water and nature lovers.

Anse Feuillard: One of the several hidden beaches along the eastern coast, Anse Feuillard is known for its powdery white sand and clear water. While this paradise is beautiful, it is also secluded and will have no amenities.

Take a moment to read the following table for a listing of beaches that can be found on the island.

BEACHES ON MARIE GALANTE		
Name	Location	Coast
Anse Canot	1.5 mi. North of Central Saint Louis	North West
Anse Chalet	0.6 mi. North of Central Saint Louis	West
Anse Feuillard	8.4 mi. East-Northeast of Central Grand-Bourg	East

Anse Taliseronde	8.2 mi. East-Northeast of Central Grand-Bourg	East
Anse de Mays	0.1 mi. Northwest of Central Saint Louis	West
Anse de l'Eglise	3.4 mi. North-Northeast of Central Saint Louis	North
Petite-Anse	4.5 mi. Southeast of Central Marie-Galante	South East
Plage de Folle Anse	2.1 mi. South West of Central Saint Louis	West

Keep in mind that Marie Galante has other attraction types. You can read on "Attractrion" pages in this book which is all about even more attractions if you're looking for additional facts.

Plage de Folle Anse

Located on the outlying island of Marie Galante, Plage de Folle Anse is known as a beach for simply relaxing.

While visitors will be able to play in the sand and on the water, the sun, the view, and the gentle breeze beckons for you to lay down and let go.

Located on the western side of the island of Marie-Galante, 2.1 miles south west of Saint Louis, You should consider stopping by even if you aren't staying in the vicinity. Travelers who make a stop at this beach will be able to escape the city's bustle without sacrificing the chance to meet new people.

How to Access The Beach
When on the island of Marie Galante, simply follow the coastal road D-206. Plage de Folle Anse is located between Anse La Frais and Ansa Ballet.

Amenities and Ambiance
Unfortunately, you won't find any public restrooms along this coastline.

If you usually desire beach days which bring guests a peaceful haven, then a good choice for you is Plage de

Folle Anse; it's tucked away within a much quieter part of Marie-Galante.

What's Nearby

Attractions

This pleasant stretch of sand known as Plage de Folle Anse is on the West coast of Marie-Galante. Delices de Siblet Sugar Factory is one of a few area's attractions.

Museums and beaches may seem an odd combination to some, but a quite a few vacationers find that museums like Ecomussee de Marie Galante (located four miles to the southeast) offer rare insight into Caribbean life and help visitors understand Guadeloupe's interesting past.

With a selection of nearby activities, you'll never get bored. The following table contains a list of nearby attractions.

ACTIVITIES AND ATTRACTIONS NEAR PLAGE DE FOLLE ANSE

Marie Galante Island Travel and Tourism

Attraction	Type	Distance	Direction	Island
Delices de Siblet Sugar Factory	Historical Site	2.8 mi.	SSE	Marie-Galante
Jardin de Buckingham	Botanical Garden	3.0 mi.	SE	Marie-Galante
Distillerie Poisson	Distillery	3.1 mi.	SE	Marie-Galante
Distillerie Poisson	Operating Distillery	3.1 mi.	SE	Marie-Galante
Poterie Au Grés Des Iles	Ceramics and Pottery Shop	3.4 mi.	SSE	Marie-Galante
Jardin de l'Habitation Murat	Botanical Garden	3.5 mi.	SSE	Marie-Galante
Ecomussee de Marie Galante	Museum	4.2 mi.	SE	Marie-Galante
Rhum Belle Distillery	Operating Distillery	5.2 mi.	E	Marie-Galante
Rhum Belle Distillery	Distillery	5.2 mi.	E	Marie-Galante

Cities and Towns

The nearest part of Marie-Galante to Plage de Folle Anse is Saint Louis. This friendly part of Marie-Galante is only two miles from the beach, so a visit doesn't need to take up the whole day. Saint Louis is an area with plenty to do, but yet isn't overcrowded.

Hotels

The mood here social and lively, or virtually empty will depend on if you visit during a popular season, which is often indicated by how busy the hotels are. This beach is not near many large hotels, but it's sometimes enjoyed by visitors staying at some of the area's smaller options.

Vacationers will find a good selection of hotels to pick from in the vicinity of Plage de Folle Anse. The most accessible of which are listed in the table below.

Marie Galante Island Travel and Tourism

ACCOMMODATIONS NEAR PLAGE DE FOLLE ANSE			
Hotel	Distance	Direction	Type
Village de Menard	3.3	NNE	Cottages
Hôtel Solédad	3.4	SSE	Hotel
Coco Beach Resort	5.3	SE	Resort

Food

Though this spot isn't close to many restaurants, you'll still have some choices, particularly if you are prepared to venture a little farther away. One of the nearest places to eat is Le Maria-Galanda, which is two miles to the northeast of it.

Restaurants closest to this beach are listed below.

RESTAURANTS NEAR PLAGE DE FOLLE ANSE					
Restaurant Name	Phone	Cuisine	Style	Distance	Direction
Le Maria-	(059)	Creole	Informal	2.1 mi.	NE

Galanda	097-5056				
Aux Plaisirs des Marins	(059) 097-0811	Creole	Very Casual	2.5 mi.	NNE
Le Murato	(059) 046-0651	Italian	Very Casual	3.4 mi.	SSE

Other Beaches

Of course, there are more fantastic beaches besides Plage de Folle Anse on Marie-Galante.

You might also want to visit Anse Chalet, located only a short distance away.

Guadeloupe has some unforgettable natural wonders to explore, and Plage de Folle Anse is just one of the many options.

Petite-Anse

Soak up some sun on the beach or head out to deeper waters for a magnificent scuba diving excursion. Scuba trips depart from the shores three times each day. However, the water is so clear that you will be able to explore underwater just by snorkeling or swimming.

Set on the island of Marie-Galante, You might want whether or not you're staying in the immediate vicinity. A surprisingly wide range of visitors end up loving Petite-Anse; it's not too far off the beaten path, plus it's never really too crowded. If you're not interested in Guadeloupe's completely quiet and hidden beaches, but don't want to fight the crowds every step of the way, Petite-Anse is worth a visit.

Amenities and Ambiance
Of course, there is also a restaurant located right on-site. There are a lot of dining experiences to be had in Guadeloupe, but having a meal on the beach can be especially enjoyable. Ask your hotel about picnic

lunches, as some hotels offer to pack snacks for their guests' day trips. Otherwise, there are plenty of walk-up vendors that offer hot, on-the-go food.

Even if you plan to dine elsewhere, the snack bar on-site could come in handy. You may also have the option to order lunch from one of the mobile vendors who typically operate along this coastline.

Restrooms are available at Petite-Anse. You'll also find umbrellas and chairs here, so guests looking for a break from the hot sun will not go leave unhappy. The water here is clear and good for snorkeling, so grab some equipment if you're hoping to see what lies beneath the surface. Petite Anse is a popular beach among sunbathers and scuba enthusiasts, so there's a good mix of interests.

the area surrounding Petite-Anse is rarely very crowded, This means that pay little attention the time of day you visit, as there is a minimal chance that you have to contend with the other tourists who might want access to the amenities found here.

What's Nearby

Attractions
Set on the South East coast of Marie-Galante; the area hosts attractions such as Rhum Belle Distillery, which is one of the most conveniently accessible attractions.

If you want to combine a little culture with your trip to the beach, you might want to consider visiting Ecomussee de Marie Galante, a lovely museum found five miles to the west, so it could be a welcomed alternative to hot afternoon activities.

Being able to choose from some activities besides the beach will ensure you won't run out of things to do. The following table contains a list of nearby attractions.

ACTIVITIES AND ATTRACTIONS NEAR PETITE-ANSE				
Attraction	Type	Distance	Direction	Island

Rhum Belle Distillery	Distillery	3.0	NW	Marie-Galante
Rhum Belle Distillery	Operating Distillery	3.0	NW	Marie-Galante
Ecomussee de Marie Galante	Museum	5.1	W	Marie-Galante
Jardin de Buckingham	Botanical Garden	5.7	W	Marie-Galante
Distillerie Poisson	Distillery	5.8	W	Marie-Galante

Cities and Towns

The nearest section of Marie-Galante to Petite-Anse is Grand-Bourg. This friendly part of Marie-Galante is only six miles from the coast, which means a trip here doesn't have to take all day. This region in Guadeloupe is a region with interesting things to do, yet is never overly congested.

Hotels

The crowdedness of the shoreline can vary widely, depending on everything from the time the sun sets to how packed the nearby hotels are. There are not many major hotels nearby, but you may see guests staying at the few small lodgings in the area.

Vacationers will find a fairly good assortment of accommodations to choose from in the vicinity of the beach. The closest of which can be viewed in the table below.

ACCOMMODATIONS NEAR PETITE-ANSE			
Hotel	Distance	Direction	Type
Résidence Cap Reva	0.1 mi.	NW	Hotel
Le Soleil Levant	0.4 mi.	N	Guest house
La Rose du Brésil	1.3 mi.	SW	Hotel
Hôtel La Souricière	2.5 mi.	WSW	Hotel
Coco Beach Resort	4.3 mi.	W	Resort
Hôtel Solédad	--	--	Hotel

Village de Menard	8.5 mi.	NW	Cottages

Food

While this location isn't located in the culinary epicenter of the area, you can still find some interesting eateries, particularly if you're prepared to venture a little out of the way. One of the closest places to eat is **Le Touloulou**, which is less than a mile to the south west of it.

Nearby restaurants are listed below.

RESTAURANTS NEAR PETITE-ANSE					
Restaurant Name	Phone	Cuisine	Style	Distance	Direction
Le Touloulou	(059) 097-3263	Creole	Very Casual	0.9 mi.	SW
La Playa	(059) 093-	Caribbean	Very Casual	1.0 mi.	SW

	6610				
Manman'dlo La Sirene	(059) 097-5743	Caribbean	Informal	1.3 mi.	SW

Other Beaches

Of course, you'll find other beaches besides Petite-Anse on Marie-Galante.

Another location you may want to try is Plage de Folle Anse, which is located within the range of a cab.

Maybe Petite-Anse is a perfect spot for you to kick back, and at the same time perhaps not the the ideal fit; in which case you should find a beach with a seclusion factor that suits you.

Anse Feuillard

One of the several hidden beaches along the eastern coast, Anse Feuillard is known for its powdery white sand and clear water. While this paradise is beautiful, it is also secluded and will have no amenities.

Located on the eastern side of the island of Marie-Galante, 8.4 miles east-northeast of Grand-Bourg, You might want whether or not you're staying in the immediate vicinity. This beach is not just beautiful, it's special in that it's one of the few quiet beaches in Guadeloupe. While Anse Feuillard may be a little farther away, it permits unparalleled relaxation opportunities.

How to Access The Beach
There is no easy way to reach this remote beach. You will have to take the main road all the way to the east side of the island, and then turn off on the side road that takes you to the coast. Finding the exact side road can be tricky, so it is suggested you have a guide, taxi service, or at least a high-quaility GPS to help guide you.

Amenities and Ambiance

There are many beautiful beaches along the island's eastern coast, but Anse Feuillard stands as one of the prettiest. Between the turquoise water, white sand, and lush green vegetation serving as a backdrop, this is a quintessential beach that people picture when they think of remote Caribbean islands. Just remember that as you wade in the clear shallow water, the beach is directly on the Atlantic Ocean, so currents and waves have the potential of becoming stronger than other places in the island chain.

Keep in mind that restrooms won't be found on-site.

Anse Feuillard brings guests an angelic and peaceful getaway, as the location that surrounds the beach is not heavily urbanized.

What's Nearby

Attractions

Beachgoers will find Anse Feuillard on the East coast of Marie-Galante. It is close to Rhum Belle Distillery, which is one of a few attractions in the region.

Beaches and museums may seem an odd combination to some, but plenty of visitors find that museums like Ecomussee de Marie Galante(situated eight miles to the west-southwest) offer a fun learning experience and help share a different side of Guadeloupe.

Beaches are nice for a few hours here and there, but there's plenty else to see during your stay. The following table contains attractions that are the closest.

ACTIVITIES AND ATTRACTIONS NEAR ANSE FEUILLARD				
Attraction	Type	Distance	Direction	Island
Rhum Belle Distillery	Distillery	4.3	W	Marie-Galante
Rhum Belle	Operating	4.3	W	Marie-

Distillery	Distillery			Galante
Ecomussee de Marie Galante	Museum	7.8	WSW	Marie-Galante
Jardin de Buckingham	Botanical Garden	7.9	WSW	Marie-Galante
Distillerie Poisson	Distillery	8.1	WSW	Marie-Galante

Cities and Towns

The nearest region of Marie-Galante to Anse Feuillard is Saint Louis. This location is only eight miles from the coast, meaning you needn't use up an entire day here. Saint Louis is not an overly urbanized area, but still has its fair share of things to do.

Hotels

Whether this spot is full of bodies or practically empty will depend on many factors, including the capacity of nearby hotels. The area is not home to many major hotels, but it can appeal to visitors from some of the smaller accommodations in the area.

Beach-goers will find a decent selection of accommodation options to pick from in the area that surrounds the beach. The most convenient of which can be seen in the table that follows.

ACCOMMODATIONS NEAR ANSE FEUILLARD			
Hotel	Distance	Direction	Type
Le Soleil Levant	3.2	SW	Guest house
Résidence Cap Reva	3.5	SW	Hotel
La Rose du Brésil	4.7	SW	Hotel

Food

Though the area surrounding Anse Feuillard isn't exactly a culinary hot spot, you can still satisfy your hunger, especially if you are willing to venture a little farther away. One of the closest places to eat is Le Touloulou, which is a quick car or cab ride away.

The table below lists dining options located near this beach.

RESTAURANTS NEAR ANSE FEUILLARD					
Restaurant Name	Phone	Cuisine	Style	Distance	Direction
Le Touloulou	(059) 097-3263	Creole	Very Casual	4.3 mi.	SW
La Playa	(059) 093-6610	Caribbean	Very Casual	4.5 mi.	SW
Manman'dlo La Sirene	(059) 097-5743	Caribbean	Informal	4.7 mi.	SW

Other Beaches

There are multiple beaches to discover on Marie-Galante, of course, so Anse Feuillard is just one of your options.

Another location you might enjoy is Anse de Mays, located within cab range of the beach. Others might prefer Anse Taliseronde, which offers more action, and is closer to other tourist hot-spots. It's found a half mile to the south.

You may also want to consider Petite-Anse, which is located three and a half miles to the south west. Petite Anse is a great place to kick back and relax on the sunny beach or depart on a scuba adventure.

Of course, Guadeloupe has hundreds of natural wonders to discover, but Anse Feuillard is both a refreshing place to relax, and a beautiful natural attraction.

Anse de l'Eglise

Enjoy canoeing in the fresh water alongside the beach or hike through the mangrove swamp. Anse de l'Eglise is a great place for water and nature lovers.

Located on the island of Marie-Galante, near Saint Louis, You might want even if you aren't staying in the vicinity. You will generally find the beach to be rather roomy, as the beach and the surroundings that call it home are not overflowing with tourists.

Amenities and Ambiance

Situated on the west coast of the island, Anse de l'Eglise is north of Saint Louis. The beach features clear blue water and also borders a body of fresh water and a mangrove swamp.

The concession stand on-site could come in handy, even if you plan to have lunch elsewhere. You might also have the option to order lunch from one of the mobile vendors who typically operate along this coastline.

Travelers can take advantage of the available picnic tables, which are perfect for setting up your carry-out food, or just lounging under the sun.

Unfortunately, you won't find any public restrooms along this coastline. Anse de Vieux Fort is a quiet, secluded beach that never gets too crowded. It's easy to find a cozy spot all to yourself.

Anse de l'Eglise's location is rarely very crowded, Taking that into consideration, you can give less thought to what part of the day you visit, since there's only a very little chance that you need to navigate around any other beach-goers who might need access to the amenities and services located here.

What's Nearby

Attractions

Visitors will find this beach on the North coast of Marie-Galante; the area hosts attractions such as Rhum Belle Distillery, which is easily reached by taxi to the south-southeast of this spot.

If you want to mix culture with your visit to the beach, you might want to consider visiting Ecomussee de Marie Galante. It's located relatively close to Anse de l'Eglise, so it would be an easy side trip to take after some time in the sun.

Beaches are one type of attraction you can visit, but there's even more to see during your stay. The following table includes the closest attractions.

ACTIVITIES AND ATTRACTIONS NEAR ANSE DE L'EGLISE				
Attraction	Type	Distance	Direction	Island
Rhum Belle Distillery	Operating Distillery	6.3	SSE	Marie-Galante
Rhum Belle	Distillery	6.3	SSE	Marie-

Distillery				Galante
Jardin de Buckingham	Botanical Garden	7.3	S	Marie-Galante
Delices de Siblet Sugar Factory	Historical Site	7.4	S	Marie-Galante
Distillerie Poisson	Distillery	7.5	S	Marie-Galante

Cities and Towns

The nearest section of Marie-Galante to Anse de l'Eglise is Saint Louis. Saint Louis is in an area with interesting things to do and see, but isn't as sprawling and crowded as some other areas.

Hotels

The number of other people sharing spots in the sand can vary widely, it depends mainly on when you visit, and how many people have booked nearby hotels. There are not many large hotels nearby, but you may encounter guests staying at some of the area's smaller options.

You'll find a decent selection of places to stay within driving distance. A list of the closest possibilities have been displayed in the following list.

ACCOMMODATIONS NEAR ANSE DE L'EGLISE			
Hotel	Distance	Direction	Type
Village de Menard	2.3	SW	Cottages
Hôtel Solédad	8.0	S	Hotel
Le Soleil Levant	8.6	SE	Guest house

Food

While this spot isn't close to many restaurants, you can still find some interesting eateries, especially if you're prepared to venture a little farther away. The closest places to grab a bite to eat is Aux Plaisirs des Marins, which is easily reached by taxi to the south west of it.

The following table lists restaurants closest to this beach.

RESTAURANTS NEAR ANSE DE L'EGLISE					
Restaurant Name	Phone	Cuisine	Style	Distance	Direction
Aux Plaisirs des Marins	(059) 097-0811	Creole	Very Casual	--	--
Le Maria-Galanda	(059) 097-5056	Creole	Informal	3.4 mi.	SSW

Other Beaches

Of course, Anse de l'Eglise is just one of many beaches you might like on Marie-Galante.

You might also want to visit Anse Canot, which is located a short distance away to the south west. Travelers seeking an unspoiled Caribbean beach with no crowds need look no further than Anse Canot.

You may find that Anse de l'Eglise is a great fit for your vacation, but maybe you want to see more; in which case there are other beaches (and other outdoor attractions) worth trying.

Anse Canot

In addition all of the regular beach activities, visitors to Anse Canot can enjoy a variety of water sports off the coast of Anse Canot. There are no facilities, however, so be sure to bring your own supplies.

Positioned on the northwestern side of the island of Marie-Galante, in the vicinity of Saint Louis, You might think about stopping by whether or not you're staying very close. The surrounding area isn't very urbanized, however, that is not to say you won't find things to do here.

Amenities and Ambiance

Many visitors find themselves ordering a drink or snack from the concessions here, even if they move off-site for lunch. You might also have the option to get lunch from one of the mobile vendors who are typically found at this location.

Unfortunately, public restrooms aren't available, so those of you traveling with small children may want to consider another spot. Due to the rusticness of the island and its accomodations, the tourist industry has not become over-crowded like most Caribbean destinations. This means the beaches, including Anse Canot, are pristine and never cramped.

Anse Canot grants an angelic and serene haven, especially since the location that surrounds the beach is positioned apart from more urban areas.

What's Nearby

Attractions

Visitors will find this beach on the North West coast of Marie-Galante. It is near some interesting sites like Rhum Belle Distillery, which is a short taxi ride away, and it is one of a few popular spots in the area.

If you want to discover more interesting facts about the history of Guadeloupe, some of the nearby attractions offer a historical perspective of the country. One of the nearest historical attractions is Delices de Siblet Sugar Factory, which is only a brief cab ride away.

With the choice of exciting activities nearby, you'll never run out of things to do. The following table contains a list of the closest attractions.

ACTIVITIES AND ATTRACTIONS NEAR ANSE CANOT				
Attraction	Type	Distance	Direction	Island
Rhum Belle Distillery	Operating Distillery	5.6	SE	Marie-Galante

Rhum Belle Distillery	Distillery	5.6	SE	Marie-Galante
Jardin de Buckingham	Botanical Garden	5.7	S	Marie-Galante
Delices de Siblet Sugar Factory	Historical Site	5.7	S	Marie-Galante
Distillerie Poisson	Distillery	5.8	S	Marie-Galante

Cities and Towns

The closest part on Marie-Galante to Anse Canot is Saint Louis. Saint Louis is a neat region that strikes a balance between island tranquility and urbanization.

Hotels

Whether or not you encounter many other people will vary depending on the time of day, particularly in the high season when hotels overflow with tourists. The beach is not located close to many large hotels, but you may meet visitors from the few small lodgings in the area.

You'll find a reasonably varied selection of hotels within driving distance. Some of the closest options have been displayed in the list below.

ACCOMMODATIONS NEAR ANSE CANOT			
Hotel	Distance	Direction	Type
Village de Menard	0.2	SW	Cottages
Hôtel Solédad	6.3	S	Hotel
Coco Beach Resort	7.5	S	Resort

Food
While this spot isn't close to many restaurants, you'll probably still spot a few places to try, especially if you are prepared to drive or bike a few miles. One of the nearest restaurants is Aux Plaisirs des Marins, which is just a short distance away.

The following table lists dining options located near this beach.

RESTAURANTS NEAR ANSE CANOT					
Restaurant Name	Phone	Cuisine	Style	Distance	Direction
Aux Plaisirs des Marins	(059) 097-0811	Creole	Very Casual	--	--
Le Maria-Galanda	(059) 097-5056	Creole	Informal	1.5 mi.	S

Other Beaches

Of course, there are lots of other spots along the coast of Marie-Galante, so if Anse Canot doesn't suit you, you can still find a great spot.

You may also enjoy Anse Chalet, another great beach choice in Guadeloupe.

You may find that Anse Canot is a great fit for your

vacation, but maybe you want to see more; in which case there are other beaches (and other outdoor attractions) worth trying.

www.ingramcontent.com/pod-product-compliance
Lightning Source LLC
Chambersburg PA
CBHW021113080526
44587CB00010B/497